The Filament

Finding Fulfillment

You are light —

Shine bright

Dianne

The Filament

Finding Fulfillment

By

Dianne Adair

𝕾𝖍𝖎𝖉𝖆𝖆𝖓𝖎𝖐𝖊𝖎

TORONTO

SHIDAANIKEI PUBLISHERS INCORPORATED – INCORPORATED IN CANADA
WWW.SHIDAANIKEI.COM
COVER DESIGN BY Dileen Simms, dileensimms.com.
Cover Image: jannoon028/Freepik.com

LIBRARY AND ARCHIVES CANADA CATALOGUING IN PUBLICATION

Library and Archives Canada Cataloguing in Publication

Title: The filament: finding fulfillment / Dianne Adair.

Names: Adair, Dianne, author.

Description: Poems.

Identifiers: Canadiana 20210097922 | ISBN 9781999225728

(softcover)

Classification: LCC PS8601.D33 F55 2021 | DDC C811/.6—dc23

PUBLISHED & PRINTED IN CANADA, 2021

Praises

"A captivating literary lighthouse!" That's my impression of this poetic collection. The words, images, and sentiments expressed in *The Filament,* grab hold of the heart. They elevate the gaze upward to behold the stunning beauty of the only One in whom true fulfillment is found. You will enjoy a feast for spiritual sustenance with "Soul Food," a journey into redemption with "Pieces at Peace," and get ignited for purpose with "Passion." It doesn't end there, dig in for more!

Rev. Marva Tyndale, Director
Real Identity Discovery Ministries.

This collection of poems is an expression of love. It reflects an unwavering appreciation for, and faith in God and His grace. The poet, Dianne Adair states that she is "mesmerized by His handiwork." The omnipresence of God is illustrated in the picturesque depictions of nature and the symbolism portrayed in "Beauty," "Dance" and "Mesmerized."

Adair reveals her personal relationship with God, depicted throughout the anthology, but particularly in "Just You and Me." The poet compares this relationship to a gift that has been "Unwrapped." In "Pieces at Peace" Adair highlights God's ability to solve "the puzzle of our brokenness," which is solidified by her trust in Him. Praise, patience and faith are the key fibers that weave and bind *The Filament: Finding Fulfillment.*

Dr. Lesley-Gail Atkinson Swaby
Founder and Managing Director, Plum Valley Publishing Ltd., Jamaica.

In *The Filament: Finding Fulfillment,* Dianne Adair urges readers to embrace the practice of consistent, active reflection. Beyond the noise—and with courageousness in tow, Adair insists that there exists enough to fill a lifetime's curiosity. Observe and learn, or wander without inhibition; the choice is yours.

Amani Bin Shikhan
Freelance Culture Writer and Producer.

Dedicated to:

Bobbi

and Maleik

Be the Light

Other books by the author

Shadows: Poetry, Tributes and Reflections (2021).

Acknowledgements

My thoughts, poems and words encompass the intricacies of life. The essence of my pen to paper is to enlighten, give hope to others and most of all, to honor my Savior, Lord and friend. The creator has allowed me to create. It is such a privilege to write to Him, with Him and for Him. It is truly beyond words to be a witness of His mercy, grace and continued favor in my life. My collection of poems has been on paper for many years. Finally, they have been published to bless as many people as possible.

My family has been patient and encouraging as they endured my "listen to this or listen to that" requests. My daughter and recipient of my constant invasion of her time and space, has been wonderful in accommodating me. Bobbi, I am grateful for your patience and your insight. Thank you to my family, Robert my husband, Maleik my son, my parents Norma and Trevor and my sister Monique. I am grateful for your love and support and for being my testers.

To my dear friends, Donna, Wilda, Elsa, Maxine, Pat, Dileen, Shellie and many others, thanks for your continuous prayers and for pushing me to take my journey on the road and to the skies. A special thank you to my dear friend Emily, whose constant nudging, encouragement and prayers to share my thoughts with you, finally came through.

I love you all and thank God for the perseverance to bring these written pieces to completion. To Christ, I give all the praise and glory because without Him I am nothing. He is my creator, my beginning and my end.

Preface

The first chapter, **About Him,** is all about God and His relationship with mankind and creation. I see Him in everything-nature, people and situations, and expressing the love and grace that flow through Him to us is a wonderful experience.

He will always be with us if we allow Him. The opportunity to pray to Him and express our joy, pain or admiration for who He is, and for what we have or do not have in this life, are conversations to be cherished as seen in the second chapter titled **Praise.**

The third chapter titled **Reflection** gives us the opportunity to reflect on our lived experiences, allows us to learn and grow in wisdom and knowledge, and to impart the lessons learned. Reflections in life will allow us to give thanks for everything, and create avenues to do better and walk in future pathways with confidence and trust.

Darkness to Light

I have always disliked the dark. As a young girl growing up in Jamaica, whenever the light went off as it so often did, I felt like my breathing was being stifled. I would scream for my mom to bring the light, the lamp with the "Home Sweet Home" logo written on it. Just a flicker of its light was a sign of life and I would stare at it until I fell asleep or the power restored.

Life can be dark. The storms we face can be overpowering and we feel like they are suffocating every aspect of our life. However, with even a glimmer of light, hope arises and cuts through the darkness, as we fight to breathe and to survive.

I can't say I will ever get used to the darkness when the power is out, but since I made Christ the source of power in my life, I know when the threatening waters rage, He is always there. I am secured in my protector and guide. He is The Light that always outshines darkness. Psalm 18:28 says, "The Lord lights my lamp. My God illuminates my darkness."

Life will never be fully bright, there will always be pockets of darkness that will try to steal our joy, peace and light. But I can always count on God to brighten my darkness and help me to see the true light, Christ.

I will lead the blind by ways they have not known,
along unfamiliar paths I will guide them;
I will turn the darkness into light before them
and make the rough places smooth.
These are the things I will do;
I will not forsake them.

Isaiah 42:16 New International Version (NIV).

CONTENTS

Introduction

There are various natural sources of light that are used to diminish or eliminate the darkness, allowing one to see clearly. According to Dictionary.com they are the sun, the moon, stars, fire and flashes of lightning. There are also living things (plants and animals) that emit light- fireflies, jelly fish and mushrooms. Then there are artificial sources of light, such as from the filament inside an incandescent light bulb that glows whenever electricity and heat run through it.

Writing about The True Light, Christ Jesus, the breath of life He has given me, and the beauty of His creations on earth, ignites my passion and a desire to express my gratitude to Him. He is the filament that lights my way from dust to dawn.

I can recall one day just sitting up in bed in a reverie. I saw from an aerial view, a community with pockets of light emanating from a few houses. The lights represented a vision of hope and life to a darkened community. I consider myself one of those lights. My motivation to write is a visceral, passionate desire to express who God is and the hope that He brings to every situation despite its darkness.

He transcends all light and I try to be a reflection of Him. We all have our own stories, heartaches and moments of immense joy that we can share. My hope is that somehow you can relate to these poems. I hope that they will invoke not just hope, life and light, but the knowledge that we share similar pathways will encourage you to never give up and continue to walk toward the light.

"Thy word is a lamp unto my feet and a light unto my path"

Psalm 119:105 King James Version (KJV).

About Him

"From dust to dawn, I am mesmerized by His handiwork."
Dianne Adair

Beauty

Your beauty is measureless
Your beauty is endless, 'Inerasable'
Expressed in this picturesque fall day
The slight chill of a crisp passing breeze
The different trees.

Clothed in an array of colors of brown
Another of yellow-dark and light
One so golden bright
This one tinged with yellow and green
Another of tangerine.

This display of colors is so vast, so distinct
Freely given to me to admire
Giving a glimpse of heaven's desire,
I look and see a white bird above
And wonder if it is a dove,

1

With my eyes focus on the sky
I see two angels praying up high,
Not far away
A gentle, firm hand, stretched out to me.

Then suddenly
Clouds cleared to reveal the blue sea of endless skies
Skies with a bright warm sun piercing my face
Giving warmth to me, to others, to the human race.

Your beauty, O' Majestic One
Is unlike any gem shone
Revealed to the eyes of man, of woman
A whiff of nature mysterious and kind
Untapped, untouched is ready to be mine!

Within and Without

I have always loved to jot down things
That come to mind
  Things about life, nature, struggle and successes
About mankind.

My heart aches when I see some things
But restored with the hope God brings,
When my days or nights
Are shaking with the cares of today
I am encouraged
When God's Words show me the way
To trust, pray and encourage others too
For one day things will become anew.

So I write to share a piece of me
Hoping my words will be a plea
For you to not give in, but to look within
To our higher power, to God, our strength and tower.

Words

You make me smile
  Sometimes laugh to tears,
Make me think
Express how I feel
Lead me on an emotional high,
Sometimes in reverie I float
Imagination travelling far
To planes I soar beyond the stars.

You inspire me, challenge me to do better
Feel better
About situations, people, life and me.

Treading cautiously
Sharing unselfishly, overtly
Whispering gently
You spur me on
To tell stories
Of good and bad, happy and sad.

Igniting feelings
Of hope, kindness, and a desire to help
Reminding me to slow down
Breathe and be more at ease.

To be gracious and kind
Not to always whine
I love to hear you, feel you, and learn from you
But that depends on me visiting
Understanding and reading you.

I need you more than you need me
To carry me through my days
To always cherish your ways
To remain clear and true to you,
To Your Words.

Security

What are you holding on to?
What are you squeezing tight
Through your days and nights?
Is it the ageless One?
The One who will
Never let go of your hand?

Let Him engulf your thoughts
Your plans, your today and tomorrows
Let go and let God Almighty
Take you to the depth of love
Of forgiveness
Of the strength you crave.

He's waiting, longing to hold you
He's your security
And no one can
Pluck you from His hands!

Would you take hold
As He extends them to you?
He walked this earth for you
Taught you
Died and rose for you
Won't you let Him in?

My Manna

My Manna is,
The privilege of awakening day to day
To feel the sunrise on my face
To rise and be on my way
To bless and be blessed as I follow His pace.

My Manna is,
The flow of the day with its challenges and all
The choice of giving Christ my daily walk
The assurance of His provisions
Despite my rise and fall
All because of His grace so tall.

My Manna is,
His protection through the day and night
As I lay reflecting on His goodness to me
As I thank Him for keeping me in sight
As He again prepares me to see.

Yours

You are my fire
You are my water
You are the one who ignites
Who douses
Who rebukes
Rewards.

You never leave me
You never forsake me
In filth and rags you picked me up
Cleansed and filled my cup
With love and grace
You made me yours
With time and trust
I grow, in your presence I bloom.

Daily I'm fed by you
Daily I'm watered
Nightly I sleep, my canopy your wings.

From dusk to dawn I'm yours
And when the morning comes
I rise, eyes wide open
Ready to be nourished
Again into your grace
Your mercy, your love
Ready to fly on your wings
For you are mine and I am yours.

Soul Food

What are you feeding your mind, your soul?
What rhythms of sounds or words?
Good or bad, happy or sad, dark or light?

Drink from the tree of life
Eat the Word
Let it absorb into the realm of your being
In your everyday life
In your dreams.

Be willing to walk the word
Talk it
Dance it
Live it
Eat and drink it!

Be the right kind of merry
It's never too late to eat or drink right
And correct your diet of life.

My Cup

When I'm dry
Your words quench my thirst
They fill me up,
Sometimes timely
And another full force.

The urgency of my need
Is receptive to your living water
As you pour,
My heart begins to tick again
Slowly,
Steadily the beats of hope resurrect
As your blood flows
To my receptive body,
Mind and soul.

Your Word is life to me
It's grace beyond understanding
Life revitalized and ready
To be filled when emptied again.

The Time

Take heed
   Today is here
      Tomorrow may never appear
A time is coming.

His love and grace are in the present
Take them now before they pass
Cross to the last day
When chances are dry
When judgment is nigh.

Creation to revelation
Have been many years in the making
The sun may never rise
The Son gives no surprise
A time is coming
Don't wait!
It will be too late.

You've been loved from above
You've been given enough time here
Bid Him near
The time has come.

Waiting

What are you waiting for?
It's not boring over here
We have more fun
Than you ever dreamed of
Clean, pure, unadulterated life of peace.

Knowing that
Our fruits are not blight with hate
Selfishness or pride
But a joy that encircles this life
Peeping into the forever
Beyond the skies.

What are you waiting for?
Until free of smoke or care
Sins of the flesh, or guilt?
That's why He came
For the sick!

That's why
He died and resurrected
The time is ripe
Waiting may wipe you out!

Pursuit

When I insulted you
With my words, my flesh, and my sins
You forgave me.

When I deliberately avoided you
Because of shame
Or fear to see the real me
You waited for me
You showed me your blood
Your sacrifice
Your crown of thorns.

When I deliberately
Put you on the back burner
You pursued me relentlessly
Your love and grace favored me
Despite my stench you never leave me.

You hover
You stretch out your hand
And show me your heart of compassion
Your passion of pursuit overwhelms me.

Words can't express my gratitude
Your indescribable love and mercy
You broke me to find you, my true love
Unconditionally
I owe you my life
And to you my life, I give
Totally!!!

Renewed Hope

When the blood drains from my face
When I feel I can't go on any more
I hear you whisper
You whisper to me in song.

In the stillness
You soothe my weary soul
As I bask in the sweetness of your spirit
Joy overcomes me
As you remind me
That you're the ageless one.

You know me inside out
You love me endlessly
Then you color my face
As streams of hope
Flow to my feeble soul rising high.

As I step towards restoration, my voice lifts
My countenance beams to attract, to inspire
I receive as I give, radiance, admiration
And love to a higher power.

Crossroads

Where are you at?
Neither coming nor going
Standing in one spot, you muse
Should I take this shot of crossing over?
Over to a side already cleared
With blood, sweat and stain
A path that still remains open?

Springs of the hope of salvation flood
Mixed emotions, fears and doubts
Choices to make.

What will make me eternally free?
It's knowing thee
The Savior who bridges the divide
The guide
Whose pain,

Tears and unfathomable love
Bridged the gap forever with His Blood
A perfect lamb
Sacrificed for me despite who I am.

His cross became my precious mat
The walk over to eternal love
Life lost no more
No longer at Crossroads.

The best walk of my life
I no longer feel the knife
Tearing at my mind, body and soul
For God rescued and made me whole.

So what about you?
The door is open wide
For you to receive Jesus Christ.

Pieces at Peace

Is it not by grace and mercy
We heal life's bruises
Salved with His Words of comfort?

That we overcome death
With the breath of His love?
That we demolish darkness
And shame with His light and hope of salvation?

Is it not a triumph when we're rewarded with time?
Time to share our gifts, despite our failures?
To resurrect our dreams
Through prayer, patience and faith
Through God's amazing grace?

Is it not beautiful to see
How He overturns our insecurities?
Our feelings of insignificance?

Piece by piece
He puts together
The puzzle of our brokenness
To give hope
To heal
To become whole
As our bodies heal
Minds and souls restored
Pieced together
With His seamless love and peace.

Only Time

You wonder when it will all end
Troubles, heartaches, crisis, ISIS
It seems endless!
Today you pray for peace and
Sometimes the pain will ease.

Tomorrow is hope for a better day
You pray
You say
This battle will only be for a time
But the end doesn't seem nigh
But God's Words never lie.

He promises never to leave you
But you need to believe too
His death, burial and resurrection were His love
The final sacrifice
It will be wise
To heed this great price.

You were always a part of His plan
So take His outstretched hand
Things WILL end in time.

Unwrapped

As I eagerly, gingerly
Yet hastily unravel the cloth
That enveloped my gift
I was instantly melted by the warmth
The beauty and love
That shone through His majestic face.

A gift like no other
A life that forever
Changed my life and beyond.

Like the bursting of buds
After a dreary winter
Giving way to the beauty
Of green leaves and life
To the fruits to come
So my precious gift
Birthed hope and promise
Of a renewed life
Sacred and dear.

The fullness of His gift
Of love was yet to unfold
A glimpse of 'tragedy' foretold
Yet the joy in His willing
Sacrifice was for my soul.

An innocent and happy face
A spotless lamb
My saving grace
One sweet day to be swept away
Forever with my gift,
To serve my unending days.

Foot Prints

You follow me each time I look up high
As I eye your footprints in the sky
I smile securely as you silently let me follow
But also loudly you bellow when
I divert from the path you designed
Steering me back to walk refined
In your foot prints in the sky.

Passion

What is your passion?
Where are you meant to go?
Which pathway are you taking?
Who will you help or invest in?
How will you use your gifts?
When will you do it?

Why are you waiting so long?
People are dying
People are waiting for the truth
To be told through you,
People need to be saved from fear
Hunger and despair
Will you be the one to help, to care?

Change 2008

Act out your thinking
Stop stalling, constantly
Saying you'll do
But never going through
With whatever you're planning.

Things frequently written on paper
Of what to achieve
To do or to be
Things from months and years gone by
Yet still you are not free.

Let the words fly off the paper
Landing on eager soil
On the lookout for food
To let them grow.

Act out your thinking!
Make sure it's God's right way for you
If you feel His Spirit, make a move.

Take a bold step
Nourish yourself along the way
Remember,
Rome wasn't built in a day.

Watch God work
But work with His watch
It's not always that complex
Don't get sidetracked!

Long Life

On Mother Earth
We live like no end in sight
No smell of death to thwart our plight.

Delays in prayer
To love, to forgive, or be forgiven
Thoughts of having more time
To believe in heaven.

But precious time passes quickly
Without you knowing,
Even with the delay
The almighty God is still gently calling.

Then one day, squarely it faces you
No time to run or hide
No time to prepare
The end is here.

Timeless

I feel like time's running out
Wasted
   Too short.

Swiftly it sweeps by
And I wonder where did it go?
What have I accomplished for me?

My family?
Mankind?
But then I think
You are the essence of time
Ageless
Boundless.

You are able to accomplish desires
Wants of years untapped
In no time
Like Jesus
Having done so much in earth's time
A short time.

Though I'm much older in earth's time,
I can be just in time
To be timeless.

Air

Sometimes I feel sure
Ready to plunge into action
  Into life's destiny, in your direction
But then, I come up fruitless
Doubts arise with wavering thoughts
No longer fearless.

My mind muffled
Swirling with what to do now?
In a bubble
It floats with questions of how?
Do I do this or that?
What will I have or have not?
The grass looks greener
On the other side
As others rise against the tide
And then I try again.

Try to hear your gentle
Voice encouraging me
To make the right choice
To breathe again.

Then step by step
I go into the right pathway
Dancing, speaking
And creating
As I sway to the beat of hope and life
Salvaged by love.

Praise

"Conversations with God are stored in heaven."
Dianne Adair

Just You and Me

You hold me in your fist so tight
  Never wanting
    To let me go without a fight
Only you understand my plight.

How I long to miss the sweltering abyss
Of this swirling mess
That only you can address.

I must do my part
For you to impart
The promises of time
Rewarded by your acts of kindness
Patience and overseeing love
From heaven above.

With outstretched hands below
You get ready to catch me
Before I get a blow
From the unforeseen blackness of life.

Wrapped in your embrace
I'm ready to face
The paths of the unknown.

Creator

I marvel at the works of thy hands
How exquisite!
  When I survey the beauty of this land
The trees, birds, bees, the sun and sky
My heart swells
With love and praise for my Creator.

The intricacies of it all is no surprise
But still amazes me
I can't imagine your face
But I know it's as beautiful as your mind.

I can't imagine your form
But I know it's real as the day I was born
I am oh so forever yours
But only because you became mine
I look forward to serving you forever.

To Be

To be your hands extended
To be your feet
To have your mind
Is an honor and a privilege
I don't want to waste it!

Day in and day out
I want to share you
In my talking
In my walking
In my working
In my worshiping
In my driving
In my being
To stay in line with your will
And to serve you
Is my ultimate desire.

Dear Lord Jesus
I humbly bow to you,
Yearning,
Striving,
To go where you want me,
Professionally,
Personally,
Purposely,
Wholly in your divine providence.

In Admiration

I open my heart to you my Lord, my all
Like an awakening flower
  Stretching forth its majestic petals
Welcoming the smiling sun
As it looks forward
To the surrounding beauty of the day.

I see delighted friends
Frolicking, flocking flowers,
And enjoying their natural fragrance, as
Eager artists armed with their tools
Burst with pleasure to
Capture its beauty on canvas, on film.

The pictures of the eye
Are ready to be displayed
Where one can admire or inspire
But this image is forever
Perched in the lens of my eye.

His Face

I lie prostrate before you,
My head bowed
  Not daring to look up
Your precious holy feet
I am unworthy to touch
But Oh, How I cherish the chance to!

Then I feel your loving smile upon me
And the glow of your presence
Pulling me like a magnet
As you slowly raise my head
Holding my face so gently to yours.

This gift of seeing your face
My savior and God Almighty
Showing me your grace
As my eyes meet yours
No words need be said.

I beam in awe of your light and glory
Your servant
In admiration of my Master
Lord and King.

What a privilege
To be in that moment
An honor to be your friend and servant
The sweetness of this moment
Forever and ever stilled
Yet flows unending.

Dance

I want to dance before you
To sway to the flow
  Of the wavering clouds
Against the piercing sunshine
As my soul stirs with the life of the sky,
I'm grateful
To be surrounded by your beauty
By barren branches basking in your glory.

I sit here loving you
Enjoying the taste of heaven on earth,
My imagination could not fathom
What's in store beyond the skies.

I see you,
Hear you,
And listen to your music above
As my mind dances and my body moves

To the Orchestra of Nature
Enjoying not only your mastery
But the Master
As I bask in your beauty
And swirl in your glory.

Things and People

You have given us
  The beauty of things and people
Countries, cultures, communities so diverse
Nature and people to nurture
To love and to cherish,
You think of everything for our comfort
For our enjoyment
You hold nothing back.

Our awakening to the singing bird
Or the melodious song of a choir
The touch of the cool breeze unseen,
But present,
The warmth of a human or animal embrace
Such amazing love!

So much we have been given
And so little you expect in return
Just to love and be loved

From sea to sea,
From shore to shore
To share in your amazing
Unfathomable gift of beauty and love.

Bring us back to the beginning
To what you so desire for us
To love you and all your creation,
To not only enjoy the beauty
Of things and people
But the One
Who is greater than them all.

On the Bench

Just finished another refreshing
Contemplative
   Complimentary walk.

I admired shrubs and tree brushes
Hovering over the ravine
And the grass on the walk way.

Some grass bright and green
Intermingled with dying
Ones waiting to be revived.

Never a dull footprint as I'm pleasantly
Blessed with a patch
Of flowers smiling up at me.

I see beauty among the weeds
As yellow and white dandelions
Give a bright perspective to life.

We have our weeds of pain and troubles
Like this COVID-19 and overt faces of hate
But always trinkets of gold whether in a petal
Or the blessing of bright sunshine on skin,
On welcomed plants,
On flying birds and jumping squirrels
Fauna and flora together,
Never fighting for life
As there's enough for all.

So on my bench I rest,
Enjoying nature and thanking God for His nurture,
For a wise field with carefree trees
Flowing in the crisp breeze,
As I breathe with ease
I wonder when that breath
Will be for all people like me,
Those adorned with shades of color.

Then almost immediately,
The sun brightens, reminding me
The Son knows my thoughts
And one day thoughts will become
Reality for all humans as one.

Another Day

Here I am enjoying another sunny day
Thanking God for my usual pathway
   Another day to walk, to talk
To tell God my thoughts.

I wonder,
Does the beautiful butterfly
See me as it passes by?
Do the trees remember me and whisper?
Do they quarrel with each other for space?
Pushing one out if they hover too much?
Do they like each other or share?
I wander along the trodden path,
Some more worn than others
Some alive, some dying,
Some dead.

Do they talk about me and how mean
I am to the burdened ground?
My conversations continue during COVID-19,
During a war on race and beyond.

Solid Rock

I praise you
Because I'm secure
  I'm confident
In You.

I praise you
Because I am present
In your presence
I praise you because
I am empowered in your embrace
I am strong
I am enlightened with your mind
Your creativity.

I praise you
Because I am made in your image
Beautifully and wonderfully made
Because I am steadfast in you

I am solid
As I stand on the Rock
That is you
I extol you!

Reflections

"Be true to the image staring back at you."
Dianne Adair

This Christmas, Part I

This Christmas
Things may not be bright
This Christmas
No gifts in sight
No pleasure
Of wrapping them tight
For those you love.

No turkey to eat
No treat
No mistletoe
Sometimes
No warm feelings
Or happy glow.

This Christmas
The chance to buy something
Nice for your family
Maybe a distant view
The means to do so are just too few,
But the need for assurance
For a tinge of joy within
Weighs heavily on your endurance
Your dependency on Him.

Maybe this Christmas
You'll just have to be satisfied
With the hope
With the trust of its true meaning of love
Family, friends and God above.

This Christmas
No material things for me
Only the warmth of those
I can and cannot see
This Christmas is different for me.

This Christmas, Part II

I thought
I couldn't afford a few gifts
    And even envisioned
A dim feeling because of this
But I proved myself wrong
And thankfully so.

I realized
It was not about the presents I gave
Only being with and enjoying
The company of those I love
Those I cherish with all my heart.

Those who made me happy
And laughed heartily
While eating turkey, ham, and cake
While drinking richly made sorrel
From which I could hardly stay awake!

Words could not express
The deep satisfaction
Of being with loved ones

But more so the chance of being alive
To celebrate
The true meaning of Christmas
The birth of Jesus Christ.

I Will

I will find my way
No matter what others or situations say
  No matter my age
My day will come when I will shine.

Sometimes treading slowly,
Sometimes like a very fast song I glide
In and out like a woven plan
Of an outcome that will be
A beautiful
Intricate master plan
Of my will to be.

From Haiti with Thanks

Y ou may never
   Witness the leaps of joy
    The overdue smiles
Nor the depths of gratitude
Your giving enabled
But to the motherless child
And the hopeful family
It is a prayer answered
A need fulfilled
And a desire turned into reality.

As tiny hands
Lovingly gripped stuffed toys
As deserving bodies
Were cleansed by the warm
And soothing feel of soap on skin
And as the pained and hurting
Were momentarily made well
Your giving hand
Filled with hope was there.

If only for the briefest of moments
You could have seen
The gleaming faces and
Sparkling eyes,
Then you would have known
The worth of your gift.

It is your giving
And your giving to come
That bring forth a happiness
That shines like
The face of a delighted child,
With a swollen heart
Haiti and I say, "thank you."

Imagine

I sit in my car
Before heading to work
   Enjoying the gentle patter of your tears
Sometimes heavy,
And other times ever so softly.

Tears mingled
With joy, love, sadness and blessings
A mixture of heavenly emotions
Poured upon all,
I smile at the gift of your beauty
Surrounded by a lush of green
Which only yesterday was unclothed
With just sticks of brown.

Like a flash,
You fashionably adorn the day
With an array of brightness
Of attractive colors of all sorts
I never dare to imagine.

I adore your creation
And yearn for more of your goodness,
As I bask in my surroundings
I eagerly anticipate my eternity with you
I just can't imagine.

Emotions

Your words
Are like music to my ears
They cushion every blow
Relax my face
And give me renewed hope.

They let my blood flow
Suffusing me with life
And visions of a better tomorrow.

Your words
Never fail
To rejuvenate my soul
My mind
My being.

I can relax again
Feel again, and breathe again
My gratitude for your love
Leaves me speechless,
You know my heart,
Lead me on.

Mesmerized

I stood there
In the faint morning light
   Silhouetted against the office wall
After being dropped off for work.

As I waited for the doors
To automatically unlock
I admired the beauty above,
Patches of dark clouds
With a crescent moon
And a bright morning star
Subtly fighting
The dawning of new life,
Invoking a calm and pleasant mood
A kind of calm before the storm,
I thought.

The serenity of the moment
Sank in with the
Whispers of the creator
As the once stilled
Trees swayed gently

Reminding me of
His gentle omnipresence,
A perfect picture
Of God's work of art.

Then almost before
My satiety was complete,
Like the sweetness
Of a dessert pie
The unfolding of
The screen revealed the azure skies
As sun timely and seamlessly
Replaced the moon
Ready for the noise
Of a new day.

Serenity

Above the 7th floor
I stood gazing in wonder
   And awe through a wide glass window
As beauty unfolds.

The tip of the forests' head
Paraded a perfect picture of rust
Yellow and green
Juxtaposed with towering
Erect architecture
Gazing in admiration
Of the view below.

Happy flighty birds zoom by
Amidst the majestic skyline
As it bursts forth
With a stream of pink
And blue hue from
Rays of a peeping sun.

Time froze as I
Witnessed with gratitude
The grace and love
Of the master piece
From my great creator.

The solace of this surreal stillness
The quietness of an office room
With no shuffling feet
Ringing phones or
Pitter-patter sounds
Was a breath of fresh air.

As His face shone on me
In this precious unforgettable moment
I felt His peace
His love and His sweet blessing.

Life's Seasons

It's a cold and snowy day
The first down pour of the season
    The ending of fall.

Chills of negative temperature
Seep into my flesh
Despite the warmth
Of a hot cup of tea
And a heightened thermostat.

My mind floats to my prayer list
The many requests to God
For family, friends and for my life.

Then my warm flesh
Became frozen
With the news of
A friend's dad passing,
A season of change
Although guaranteed
Psychologically,
Unprepared we are.

Time meanders
From life to death
In no time
Leaving traces of
The in-between
And memories of
Loved ones to embrace.

Human Colors

I smile at the variety
The beautiful colors of flesh-brown
  Black, tan, white, dark
And pale as they flash by,
How sightly!

Call it multi-colored,
Multicultural, multi-faceted,
Anything you like!
It's simply a beautifully
Unified masterpiece
Of the Master's creation.

A creation of the Human Being
Different yet similar
Made for His master plan
To live, to love, to serve Him.

Again

Here I am again in my spot, my corner
Trembling along with shivering trees
   In this crisp fall breeze
I admire the sheet of beautiful brown
Rust and gold shed leaves
Laden among peeping green grass
Sparkling in the glistening sun.

Already barren branches look on
Getting ready for
A season of nakedness
Ready to receive
The company of birds' nest
Taking refuge.

In the distant view
The owner of a red car captures
The beauty of it
With lens elongated and hyperopic
Rolling in the minute details of it all.

The intricacies of time
And nature live on
And with a smile, we three
Squirrel, I and the man with the second eye
Savor it all.

His Peace

Engulfed in your presence
I lay serene in your peace
Amidst turmoil and fears
Anxious thoughts engage
Ready for the
Battle of your peace.

No need to understand
How the battle is won
Even before it began
As long as He steers the boat
No raging waves or
Blackened sky can cloud
My peace.

The steady beam
Of light from above
Keep my eyes
Focused on your love.

With my heart
Receptive to your voice
You will forever fight for me
As I remain enamored,
Engulfed,
Enlightened in
Your presence of peace.

Pathway

I don't need to understand
The works of your mighty hand,
  With you in total control
Your hands will unfold
The things that need to be told.

You direct my feet
To heights unknown,
To progress
To places above and beyond,
 I exalt my God of the impossible
To reveal in time
The importance of the gospel.

Seasons' Change

Sipping my hot chocolate,
I look out my window at the hazy mist,
At the lush hilly snow
Disturbed by remnants
Of happy feet as they go.

I see unclothed tree branches
Laden with icicles as they drip,
Smiling faces, I thought, with another sip.

Drinking in the beauty of the year,
I shiver with warm thoughts of those held dear
Seasons' change-they come and go
From cold to warm
Hot to cold
A variety of life we all need to hold.

Only God knows the beauty
In mixing it up-people, life, joy, love
To that I refill my cup.